ANATOMY OF AN INVESTIGATION

Computer Science and IT:
INVESTIGATING A CYBER ATTACK

Anne Rooney

Heinemann
LIBRARY
Chicago, Illinois

© 2014 Heinemann Library
an imprint of Capstone Global Library, LLC
Chicago, Illinois

To contact Capstone Global Library please phone 800-747-4992, or visit our website www.capstonepub.com

Edited by Andrew Farrow, Adam Miller, and Adrian Vigliano
Designed by Richard Parker
Original illustrations © HL Studios
Illustrated by James Stayte (pages 4-7); HL Studios
Picture research by Ruth Blair
Production by Sophia Argyris
Originated by Capstone Global Library Ltd.
Printed and bound in China by CTPS

17 16 15 14 13
10 9 8 7 6 5 4 3 2 1

Library of Congress Cataloging-in-Publication Data
Rooney, Anne.
 Computer science and IT : investigating a cyber attack / Anne Rooney.
   p. cm.—(Anatomy of an investigation)
 Includes bibliographical references and index.
 ISBN 978-1-4329-7601-9 (hb)—ISBN 978-1-4329-7607-1 (pb)
 1. Computer crimes—Investigation. 2. Computer hackers. 3. Computer security. I. Title.

 HV8079.C65R66 2014
 363.25'968—dc23   2012034484

Acknowledgments
The author and publisher are grateful to the following for permission to reproduce copyright material: Alamy pp. 16 (© Ian Shaw), 33 (© Marmaduke St. John), 43 (© Nikita Buida), 46 (© aberCPC); Corbis pp. 11 (© DB Apple/dpa), 27 (© Corbis), 42 (© Ramin Talaie); Getty Images pp. 8 (Florence Delva), 19 (William Thomas Cain), 22 (ColorBlind Images), 25 (JIJI PRESS/AFP), 37 (Chris Jackson), 39 (Betsie Van der Meer), 40 (Alan Weller/ Bloomberg); Shutterstock pp. 9 (© Angela Waye), 12 (© Dmitry Kalinovsky), 14 (© Elena Elisseeva), 15 (© Dmitriy Shironosov), 17 (© Ermolaev Alexander), 21 (© Arno van Dulmen), 34 (© dwphotos), 35 (© Franz Pfluegl), 38 (© YanLev); Superstock pp. 13 (Ambient Images Inc.), 36 (imagebroker.net).

Cover photograph of computer hackers using a computer reproduced with permission of Corbis (© Ocean).

We would like to thank Mark Clarkson for his invaluable help in the preparation of this book.

Every effort has been made to contact copyright holders of any material reproduced in this book. Any omissions will be rectified in subsequent printings if notice is given to the publisher.

All the Internet addresses (URLs) given in this book were valid at the time of going to press. However, due to the dynamic nature of the Internet, some addresses may have changed, or sites may have changed or ceased to exist since publication. While the author and publisher regret any inconvenience this may cause readers, no responsibility for any such changes can be accepted by either the author or the publisher.

Contents

Some words are printed in bold, **like this**. You can find out what they mean by looking in the glossary on page 52.

SIGNS OF TROUBLE

What is this anyway?... Oh no! It's a scam—stealing login details.

TO VIEW THIS VIDEO ENTER LOGIN DETAILS.

USER NAME:

PASSWORD:

I hope my friends didn't fall for this. I'll delete the link from my wall.

Who's that? Better log out this time!

Hello, Jayne, come in!

KNOCK KNOCK!

Ben is soon talking with his friend, and he forgets about the problem...

How has Ben's computer been hacked? And how much damage has the hacker done? Ben will have to take his laptop into work for the IT department to investigate...

Attack!

A cyber attack is not like a burglary or a physical assault—the victim might not know immediately that it has happened or its full extent. By the time Ben spots the first clue, an attacker could have done a lot of harm to his computer.

Physical access

When Ben opens his laptop and notices his profile page has been changed, he realizes someone has had access to his account. He tries to figure out how this has happened.

If you think someone has changed your computer setup, think carefully about who might have had access to it.

The easiest way for someone to change computer **data** without permission is through physical access to the computer. Ben remembers that he left his account logged on when his friends came to visit, so perhaps someone else has used his laptop. No one needed to do anything difficult—it would have been easy for one of them to change his page if he had left it logged on to his account.

As Ben has realized, it is important not to leave a computer logged on to an account and then go away from the computer, or to leave sensitive information visible on-screen. At home or school, always log out of your account when you finish using the computer. Otherwise, the next person to use the computer can use your account. That person could send messages from your account or change or delete your work files.

Thinking like an investigator

At first, Ben wondered if a friend had used his laptop to play a joke on him. He had left it logged on, so someone could have done this. But he sees that his account has been changed again when no one else could have used his laptop, so he has to think carefully about what could have happened. If someone using a different computer has changed Ben's account, then that person must know his password. He wonders whether someone has guessed his password or watched him typing it. By changing his password when he first noticed changes, he could have stopped the person from using his account again.

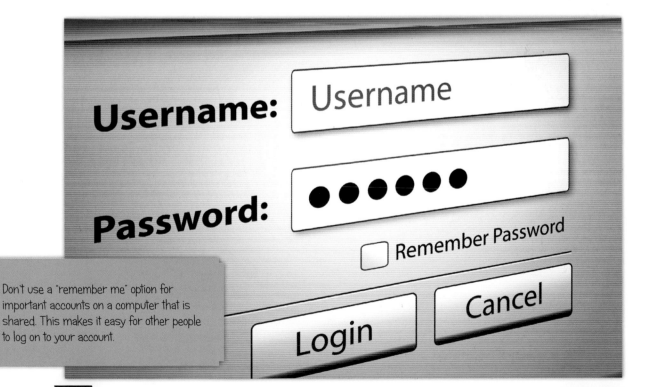

Don't use a "remember me" option for important accounts on a computer that is shared. This makes it easy for other people to log on to your account.

Cyber attacks

A cyber attack is any attack on a computer system. Cyber attacks are sometimes random—there is no particular target, and it is just bad luck if your computer is attacked. At other times, they are directed against a particular person or organization that the attacker dislikes for some reason.

Hackers and crackers

Cyber attacks are sometimes called **hacks**, meaning a **hacker** has tried to access the computer or account. A hacker is someone who breaks into computer systems illegally. Many programmers prefer the term cracker for someone who carries out criminal hacking, because hacker originally meant anyone talented at working with computers and other technology.

Hackers can be "black hat" hackers, who break into systems illegally, or "white hat" hackers, who find security loopholes so that they can then be fixed (see page 46 for more on this subject).

Hackers break into computer systems for several reasons. Some want to make money or do it for commercial gain of some sort (such as damaging a business competitor). Some enjoy the challenge of figuring out how to do it and rarely do serious damage. Others are **activists**, doing damage to bring attention to a cause or to harm an organization they do not approve of. No matter what the motive is, black-hat hacking is illegal.

Anonymous

Anonymous is a loose collection of "hacktivists"–people who use hacking to further ethical or political aims. It is not a formal organization, and anyone who wants to can take part in the group's activities.

Anonymous has been involved in several attacks against organizations fighting online piracy (illegal sharing or distributing of copyrighted material). Attacks generally take the form of **distributed denial-of-service (DDoS)** attacks. These involve setting lots of computers to access a web site at the same time. The web **server** cannot cope with the demands and crashes (stops working). In public protests in the real world, Anonymous activists wear masks.

Some famous people have been hackers. This photo shows Steve Jobs (standing) and Steve Wozniak in 1975. These men, who later founded Apple, started their partnership building blue boxes for "phone freaking," which was a way of making illegal, free phone calls. They found a way to mimic the telephone tones that signal to the system that the call is being paid for. Tim Berners-Lee (the inventor of the World Wide Web) and Linus Torvalds (the inventor of the Linux operating system) also began as hackers.

Hijacked

Ben's e-mail account has been hijacked and used to send out **spam**, or unwelcome advertising messages. A computer that is not properly protected or that uses passwords that are easy to guess can easily be taken over, becoming part of a **botnet**—a **network** of computers controlled from a distance over the Internet by a hacker. A computer used like this is sometimes called a **zombie** computer. Attackers can use the list of contacts in an address book on the computer or can mail to their own list of contacts, using the attacked computer's account details.

Botnets are often used for DDoS attacks. DDoS attacks are sometimes aimed by hackers at commercial rivals or organizations the hacker does not approve of for ethical or political reasons. It is not always obvious if a computer is part of a botnet. There might be clues—such as the computer running more slowly than normally—but sometimes a computer can be **compromised** in this way for months before anyone notices.

In 2010, a hacker named Artur Boiko was jailed in Estonia for more than two years for launching a DDoS attack against an insurance company. He did not like the company's treatment of his claim following a traffic accident.

Linked accounts

Ben's e-mail and social network accounts are separate and have different passwords, so he knows the strange e-mail message is a sign of a more serious problem.

THINKING LIKE AN INVESTIGATOR

When he finds that his e-mail is also affected, Ben is very worried. He realizes that this is not just someone guessing his password—although if he had used the same password for both accounts, that could have been the cause. The next morning, he finds that he cannot log on to either his social network or his e-mail. Whoever is using his accounts must have changed the passwords.

Many web services invite you to share your e-mail address book or other accounts with them. You can share your address book with a social networking site so that it can send your friends invitations to join, or link to services such as Twitter and Facebook so that more people see your updates. When you link your accounts, if any one of them is attacked or compromised, the others are at risk, too.

It can be very easy to select an option that synchronizes or shares your contacts and account information between applications. Think carefully before you do it, because you might be making your personal information less secure.

Keeping Information Safe

Ben is very worried, because he uses his computer for personal banking and also to work on secure projects for his job. The attack could put his bank account at risk or damage his organization's business.

Computer accounts

Ben takes his computer to the IT department at his office. He speaks to Sadia, an IT support worker. She asks him about his passwords and how he protects them.

You are probably used to having to log on to use a computer at school or to use a social networking or data sharing web site. These systems keep a list of all the people who have registered to use the system. Each person has a separate account.

To be allowed to use your data, you need to prove who you are by logging on—giving your user name and password. User names are unique—each user name can only be used by one user on the system. At school, you will probably have a user name that is something like your real name. On a web site, you can pick your own user name, as long as no one else has used it. It does not need to be anything like a real name, and it can be a good idea to pick a nickname that does not identify you clearly. You do not need to keep your user name secret.

You can think of your account as being like a locked door. The user name tells the computer which door you want to open, and the password is the key to that door. You need to use the right password for the right user name.

If someone sees you enter your password, your account is no longer secure.

Passwords do not need to be unique, but you do need to keep your password secret. If people find out or guess your password, they can log on to the computer system just as if they were you and do all the things that you can do with your accounts.

RULES FOR PASSWORDS

To pick a strong password:

- Mix capital and lowercase letters, numbers, and possibly symbols such as an ampersand (&), underscore (_), or a semicolon (;), if they are allowed.

- Don't use something other people can guess, such as your birth date or your pet's name.

- Don't use a real word. Some hackers use **software** that tries out all real words as passwords.

- Keep your password private. Choose something you can remember, so that you do not need to write it down.

- Change your password if you think someone has figured it out or guessed it.

Different passwords

Some systems insist that you change your password frequently. Some experts say you should use different passwords for every account, yet you should not write them down. It can be difficult to keep track of lots of passwords—especially if you keep changing them! So, what should you do?

Keep the password to your account safe—if you don't, it is easy for people to change or delete your files or do things in your name. They might do it as a joke, but it is not very funny when you lose your homework or get in trouble for sending nasty messages.

If you use the same password for everything and someone discovers it, that person can use any of your accounts. That is obviously not good. Many people use the same password for all the accounts that are not very important (such as logging on to a movie site to order tickets), but they use different passwords for accounts that need more security. It could be disastrous if someone used your school account or deleted all your pictures on Tumblr or—for an adult—if someone accessed an online bank account. Those accounts should each have their own passwords.

Changing your password

If someone discovers your password, you should change it immediately, to stop him or her from using your account any further—when the hacker logs on with the old password, it will not work. If Ben had changed his password at the first sign of trouble, he might have stopped further damage to his account.

You can use the "change settings" options on your account to change your password. You might get an email saying you've changed your password. It seems silly—you know you've done it! But this is to check that it's really you changing the password, and not someone who has gained access to your account. If you ever get an email saying you have changed your password when you haven't, follow it up immediately—someone might be stealing your account.

Change Password

User:

Password:

Confirm password:

Strength: Strong

| User XYZ |
| ********** |
| ********** |
| Strong |

To change your password, you usually have to type the new password twice to make sure you have typed it correctly. Some accounts also evaluate the password strength, giving an idea of how difficult the password will be to guess or discover using software. Passwords that use the names of pets or familiar names and dates are much more likely to be guessed than unusual combinations of characters that mix letters and numbers.

YOU'RE THE INVESTIGATOR!

Think of four questions you would ask Ben to help him figure out what might have happened. Some ideas are on page 18.

What if you cannot log on?

If someone discovers your password and logs on to your account, then that person can change your password. Most login pages have a link to click to reset your password or send your password to your e-mail address. You can do this to reset your password and claim back your account. But if the hacker has changed the e-mail address linked to your account, you will not get an e-mail. Then you will need to contact the help desk.

Breaking passwords

Professional hackers often use software to try to break passwords. A "brute force" attack uses a program that keeps trying different passwords. It might work through a dictionary, for example, trying each word. Because a program can do this very quickly, it can try a lot of words in a very short time.

YOU'RE THE INVESTIGATOR!: THE ANSWER

Any of these questions would be useful to ask Ben:

- Did he leave his account logged on when other people were around?
- Has someone seen him type his password?
- Has he written his password down?
- Has he used the "remember me" option on a public computer?
- Is his password easy to guess?
- Does he use the same password for everything?

Super secure

Some systems need to be especially secure. If banking, police, or defense systems are hacked, the consequences can be very serious. They often use extra checks, and even extra **hardware** such as fingerprint recognition or iris recognition (see the box and photo on page 19). These are called biometric systems. Only the person with the right fingerprint or the right eye pattern can access them.

The iris is the colored part of the eye. It has a pattern as unique as a fingerprint. Iris-recognition systems compare the eye with a stored image of the account holder's eye as a security check.

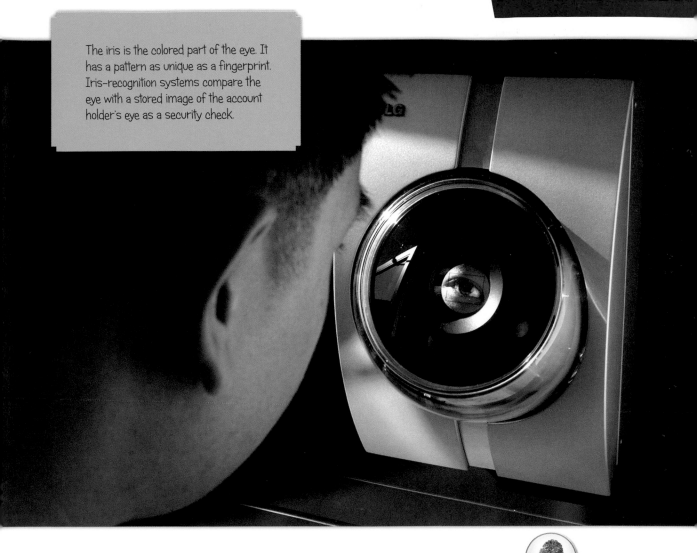

"Over my dead body"

Fingerprint recognition systems can also be used as locks to buildings, rooms, and safes. Computer scientists recognized early on that fingerprint recognition systems could be abused if a criminal cut the finger off the authorized person. Some special systems will only work if the finger is at body temperature and has a normal level of moisture from sweat, to avoid this gruesome method of hacking.

Confirming the Attack

Ben has protected his passwords, and his accounts have been accessed from outside, not using his laptop. So Sadia, the IT support worker at Ben's office, concludes that he has been the victim of a cyber attack. She is alarmed. This means that any of the organization's systems could have been attacked. She works quickly to find out the nature of the attack and what it has done.

IT SUPPORT WORKER

IT support workers help to maintain computer systems in an organization.

They need to know about computer hardware and software, to understand how computers are used in the organization, and to know the law relating to computer use. The job involves setting up computers, installing and upgrading software and hardware, setting up user accounts, running backup routines, and helping users with problems. This can be an entry-level job that people go into straight from college or sometimes with a high school degree and special classes. On-the-job training is common. Trainees need to be interested in and knowledgeable about computers.

Most malware—nearly 70%—is Trojans, which often go unnoticed for months. Viruses are the next most common type of malware, followed by worms.

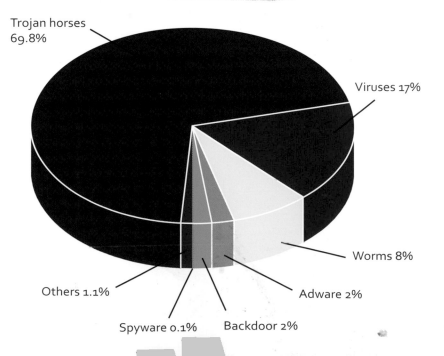

Trojan horses
69.8%

Viruses 17%

Worms 8%

Others 1.1%

Adware 2%

Spyware 0.1%

Backdoor 2%

Malware

When Ben explains to Sadia that he has kept his passwords safe, she decides that there is probably **malware** on his computer. Malware, short for "malicious software," is software intended to do harm. As we will see, there are lots of different sorts of malware, and malware is extremely common. In 2011, Microsoft estimated that 1 in every 14 **downloads** from the Internet included malware. The most common types of malware are **Trojans**, **viruses**, and **worms**.

Trojans

A Trojan has to be installed on the computer by the user, so it needs to disguise itself as something the user might want. It is often hidden inside something else, so you install it without realizing it, perhaps along with a program downloaded from the Internet.

Some Trojans install a "backdoor," which is a bit of software that allows a hacker easy access to the computer in the future, bypassing usual security checks—similar to leaving the back door of a house open. The Trojan might install **spyware**, or it might hijack the computer to use it for a bad purpose, such as sending out spam. Spyware is not usually disruptive, because it aims to go unnoticed.

Trojans are named after the legendary Trojan horse of ancient Greek legend. Ancient Greek soldiers laying siege to the city of Troy made a huge wooden horse, which they offered as a gift to the citizens of Troy. But Greek soldiers secretly hid inside the horse, and when it was dragged into the city, they leapt out and killed the Trojans.

Spyware

Spyware gathers information or "watches" what you are doing on the computer, and then it sends information to a distant computer over the Internet. It can include a **keylogger** that records everything typed—including sensitive information such as passwords. The information gathered can be used to access accounts, steal data or money, redirect web searches, or send pop-up advertisements. Malware that sends advertising to a computer is called adware. It is more annoying than harmful.

Few amateur hackers write their own code. Instead, they find chunks of software online, then they either adapt it or use it as it is.

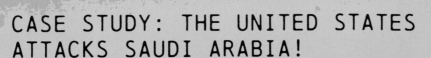

CASE STUDY: THE UNITED STATES ATTACKS SAUDI ARABIA!

In 2012, a link to a fake page for the cable news channel CNN reported that the United States had attacked Saudi Arabia. This tricked a lot of Facebook users. The link promised a video of the attack (which had not actually happened), and then opened a pop-up window prompting users to upgrade their Adobe Flash player. This was not a real upgrade. People who accepted the "upgrade" downloaded a Trojan on to their computers. Within three hours, 60,000 people fell victim to the scam.

Some Trojans include a rootkit. This software conceals the operation of the Trojan, to make it hard to detect. It changes the **operating system** to hide the Trojan's files, so that the Trojan is not included in the list of **processes** that are running.

Viruses and worms

Viruses and worms spread between computers by themselves. Most spread over the Internet, either as an e-mail attachment or hidden in a downloaded program or file.

A virus **infects** a piece of executable code (part of a computer program), and when that code is run, the virus spreads to other files. If you do not start the infected code, the virus cannot spread to affect other programs on your computer.

A worm is a program that can spread itself over a network without anyone opening or starting an infected file or program.

YOU'RE THE INVESTIGATOR!

What sort of malware do you think might be on Ben's computer? Remember that someone has gained the password to his social network account and his e-mail. The answer is on page 25.

Carrying extra

Both viruses and worms often carry a payload, which is an extra chunk of computer program that does something else, usually something bad. It might delete files on the computer or change settings, for example. Some cause only a slight disruption, but others make the computer unusable, destroying data and essential programs.

The harm that malware does

Some malware is intended to disrupt or destroy random computer systems by deleting data and programs. It is not aimed at a particular target. But a lot of malware is used for financial gain or to disrupt business operations. It might involve stealing information or money, diverting trade from one business to another, or stopping a rival from trading normally.

Stealing information can be done by hacking into a system and looking at the information stored, or by trying to trap information in transit over the Internet. Information can be used for **identity theft** or to take money from a bank account, for example. Information stolen from a business can be used to attract customers away, build rival products or services, or embarrass a business to harm it financially—customers will not continue to use an online service if their details are made public.

Details of the new product Ben is working on might have been stolen from the network using his login details. This could be disastrous, as a competitor could copy the product and bring it out first, damaging his organization's business.

Look out for phishing

A common way to steal account details and passwords from individuals is "phishing." Phishers set up a web site that looks like one people trust, such as an online banking or social networking login page. People are tricked into using the fake site by clicking on a link in an e-mail. The fake page collects the user names and passwords entered and then uses them dishonestly.

You should never follow login links from an e-mail, no matter how convincing they look. Always go to the homepage of the site and log in from there. Some phishing sites set up web sites with only one different letter from a "real" URL, hoping to catch a few people who type the address in wrong-typing "buymuisc" instead of "buymusic," for example.

A phishing web site usually looks very much like the real web site—that is how it tricks people. This fake website was set up to trick people in Japan.

SPEEDY WORM

Because worms spread without human intervention, they can spread extremely quickly. The SQL Slammer worm, released in 2003, infected 75,000 computers in 10 minutes.

YOU'RE THE INVESTIGATOR!: THE ANSWER

There is probably a Trojan on Ben's computer. A Trojan can install a keylogger, and this might be how a hacker got his account details.

Assessing the Damage

If a computer that is used to connect to a network has malware on it, it is possible that the malware has spread elsewhere on the network or has allowed an intruder to see and change files on the network. The organization has to check the whole network.

Looking for malware

Sadia tells the system administrator, Greg, that Ben's laptop has malware on it. Since Ben uses his laptop to access the organization's network, she is worried that the whole network might have been infected or compromised.

SYSTEM ADMINISTRATOR

A system administrator is a senior role taken by someone with expert IT knowledge.

The system administrator is responsible for setting up and possibly designing IT systems, planning the purchase of hardware and software and its installation, assessing performance, dealing with serious problems and security issues, deciding policy in some areas of IT use, and solving technical problems that are too difficult for junior support staff. The system administrator might also do some programming and examine **log files** to check how the system is being used. This job requires experience in IT and system administration. Many system administrators have a degree in a computer-related subject as well as several years of experience in IT support work.

Greg suspects that there is a keylogger on Ben's computer. This traps everything Ben types and sends it to a distant hacker. It could have been installed with a Trojan. He tests his theory with a deep investigation of Ben's laptop.

The laptop is running Microsoft Windows. The computer has a database called the Windows **registry**, which holds information about and settings for all the software installed on the computer, including the operating system and **applications** such as software for writing text or playing music. Greg can look at and even change the registry using special software. He has to be very careful while making any changes, because a mistake can make the computer unusable.

Looking at the registry, Greg finds entries for a couple of programs he does not recognize. One of these turns out to be a keylogger, so his theory was correct.

Serious implications

Ben uses his laptop to access the organization's network when he is working off-site. The keylogger means that a hacker has been able to trap Ben's user name and password for the network when he has logged on. The hacker could have used Ben's details to access files on the network.

System administrators are responsbile for IT systems. such as server rooms like this. They will monitor how a system is being used.

Looking at computer networks

A network links computers together so that they can share resources such as printers, servers, software, files, and Internet access. Equipment can be linked by cables, but many modern networks are wireless and use radio waves to send information.

A network in a single building or other small location is called a local area network, or LAN. A network over a larger geographic area is a wide area network, or WAN. The largest WAN is the Internet, which spans the whole world. A computer can belong to more than one network at a time. Ben's laptop connects to the Internet through the LAN at his workplace.

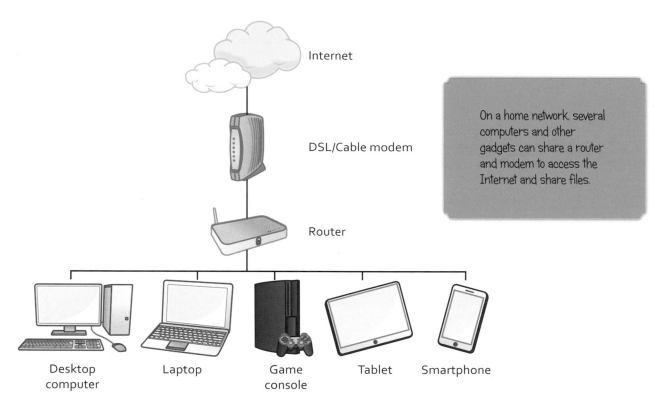

Internet

DSL/Cable modem

On a home network, several computers and other gadgets can share a router and modem to access the Internet and share files.

Router

Desktop computer   Laptop   Game console   Tablet   Smartphone

Parts of networks

A small home network might have only a few computers, a **router**, and a **modem**. A router operates like a post office, sending data where it needs to go. It takes information going from a computer to the Internet and forwards it to the modem, which controls traffic to and from the Internet. The modem connects to the Internet, passes the data on, and picks up incoming data. The router then takes information coming in from the modem and sends it to the right computer on the network. The router can also send information between computers on the local network.

A large network works in the same way, but it also has servers—powerful computers that allocate and manage resources. The physical objects that make up any computer system are called hardware.

Servers

A server is a powerful computer dedicated to a particular task. There are servers for different purposes. A web server stores web pages and "serves" them—meaning it sends them out—when they are needed. A printer server manages printers and requests for print jobs from computers on the network. Various types of network servers manage the network itself, and file servers hold work and other files.

```
PyKeylogger\logs

1    20130326|1740|C:\Program Files\Mozilla
2    Firefox\firefox.exe|262710|SoftwareInstall|Private Browsing — Mozilla
     Firefox (Private Browsing)|https://www.gmail.com[KeyName:Return]
3    20130326|1741|C:\Program Files\Mozilla Firefox\firefox.exe|262710
     |SoftwareInstall|Gmail:E-mail from Google — Mozilla Firefox (Private
     Browsing)| Ben.Cooper[KeyName:Tab] Waliaysₙays[KeyName:Return]
4    20130326|1741|C:\Program Files\Mozilla Firefox\firefox.exe|262710|
     SoftwareInstall|Gmail — Compose Mail — ben.cooper@gmail.com - Mozilla
     Firefox (Private Browsing)|caitlin.brookes2[BS]@gmail
     com[KeyName:Tab]Paying for the holiday[KeyName:Tab]Hello Caitlin!
5    20130326|1741|C:\Program Files\Mozilla Firefox\firefox.exe|262710|
     SoftwareInstall|Gmail — Compose Mail — ben.cooper@gmail.com - Mozilla
     Firefox (Private Browsing)| KeyName:Return] [KeyName:Return]Please
     pay for the holiday with my debit card, number 4649
6    20130326|1741|C:\Program Files\Mozilla Firefox\firefox.exe|262710
     SoftwareInstall|Gmail — Compose Mail — ben.cooper@gmail.com - Mozilla
     Firefox (Private Browsing)| 8929 3363 8190, exp. date 06/16,
     security
     code 267. Then you can pay me your share when you
7    20130326|1742|C:\Program Files\Mozilla Firefox\firefox.exe|262710
     SoftwareInstall|Gmail — Compose Mail — ben.cooper@gmail.com - Mozilla
     Firefox (Private Browsing)|paid. [KeyName:Return][KeyName:Return]Take
     care — Ben x
8    20130326|1742|C:\Program Files\Mozilla Firefox\firefox.exe|262710
     SoftwareInstall|Gmail — Compose Mail — ben.cooper@gmail.com - Mozilla
     Firefox (Private Browsing)|
```

YOU'RE THE INVESTIGATOR!

This is a file created by a keylogger that was found installed on Ben's laptop. Which parts do you think might be of interest to a hacker? The answer is on page 30.

YOU'RE THE INVESTIGATOR!: THE ANSWER

There are two pieces of valuable information. Ben's login details for his Gmail account are contained in the third part of the file. With this information, the hacker could use Ben's e-mail account to send out spam e-mails, could read his e-mail, or could use his list of contacts.

The hacker would also find Ben's debit card details, which are in parts five and six of the keylogger file. With this information, the hacker could buy things using Ben's debit card.

```
Ben.Cooper[KeyName:Tab]
Waliays¬ays[KeyName:Return]
and
4649 8929 3363 8190¬ exp.
date 06/16¬ security code
267
```

These fragments of the file show Ben's user name and password—Ben.Cooper and Waliays.ays—and his debit card details.

Software and security for the network

A network needs software in addition to hardware. Networking software manages network security and keeps track of users and what they are allowed to do (their access rights).

In a small business network, switches join parts of the network together and send messages between computers and to the router or modem.

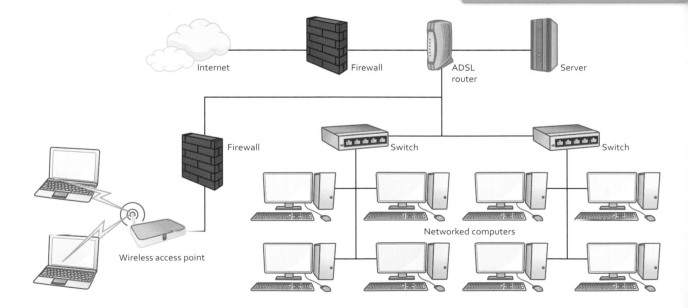

Internet · Firewall · ADSL router · Server · Firewall · Switch · Switch · Networked computers · Wireless access point

Firewalls

One important aspect of network security is keeping a secure border between the Internet and the local network. This is achieved using a **firewall**. A firewall can be a piece of hardware or software. The firewall examines all requests for access to the internal network and checks all data going out to the Internet. It assumes that the internal network is secure and trusted, but the Internet is not. It uses a set of rules to decide whether each item of traffic is allowed to pass through the firewall.

Some routers contain firewall components. Most personal computers are supplied with some security software that includes a firewall, and this is often the only firewall that you need on a home network.

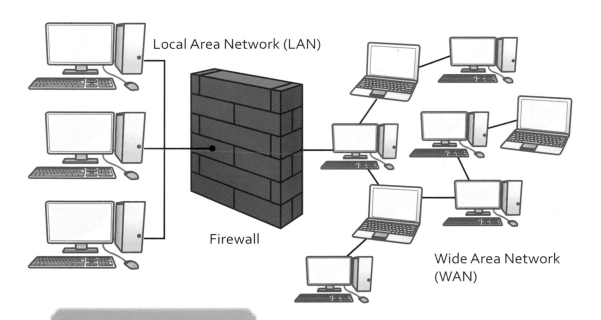

Local Area Network (LAN)

Firewall

Wide Area Network (WAN)

A firewall stands between the trusted local network and the untrusted Internet. Its function is to prevent unauthorized access to the local network.

Keeping track

Computers keep log files of activity. From these, Greg can see which processes have been active, and which user accounts have been used to access files. Greg asks the network manager, Lena, to look at activity from Ben's account. Lena can see from the log files which files have been changed, who changed them, and when. She knows Ben's typical network activity and so will easily be able to spot anything unexpected. Lena finds that many files have been changed from Ben's account. Some of these changes are genuine—they are Ben's normal work. Others are not things he would have done, and she believes a hacker made them using Ben's login details. Based on this information, Greg decides this is a serious attack and calls the police.

NETWORK MANAGER

The network manager is responsible for the smooth running of the network, including security.

This job involves installing and maintaining network hardware and software, making sure there is enough capacity for the expected network traffic, and solving problems when the network stops working or works slowly. The network manager needs to understand how networks operate, and what the security and legal issues are relating to networks. The network manager maintains the firewall and software, such as antivirus programs that protect the network. In a small organization, the network manager might also manage the web site.

```
List of files accessed from Ben.Cooper, 17:00 hours March 4th to 10:30 hours March 5th:
H:\root\design\project102\CAD\int231\upper.psd      17:15:34      update
H:\root\design\project102\CAD\int231\lower.psd      17:32:17      update
H:\root\design\project102\CAD\int231\mez.psd        17:34:29      create
H:\root\user\web\pages\offers\june.html             03:01:04      delete
H:\root\user\web\pages\offers\top.html              03:01:05      delete
H:\root\user\web\pages\offers\today.html            03:01:06      delete
H:\root\user\web\pages\contact\mailto.html          03:01:08      update
H:\root\user\web\pages\offers\june.html             03:01:11      upload
H:\ProgramData\Sage\Accounts\2014                   05:38:26      update
H:\root\design\project102\CAD\int231\mez.psd        09:24:42      update
```

YOU'RE THE INVESTIGATOR!

This is a log of activity on the network. Ben's user name on the network is Ben.Cooper. He works on product design. Which entries do you think are suspicious? See page 35 for the answer.

Data security

Individuals and organizations need to keep sensitive and valuable data secure. On home computers, sensitive data includes passwords that give access to bank accounts and perhaps personal correspondence or health records. In business systems, sensitive data includes:

- personal details of employees and other people
- financial data, including details of payments owed and due, how well the business is doing, and its banking details
- commercial information about products and services, clients, or customers and what they have bought
- plans and projections relating to future business
- Research and development documents, design drawings, and blueprints relating to possible future products or services.

Many countries have laws and regulations about what personal data can be stored by organizations. There are also laws and regulations about what information can be shared with other organizations, and how information must be held securely, especially by financial institutions and providers of health care.

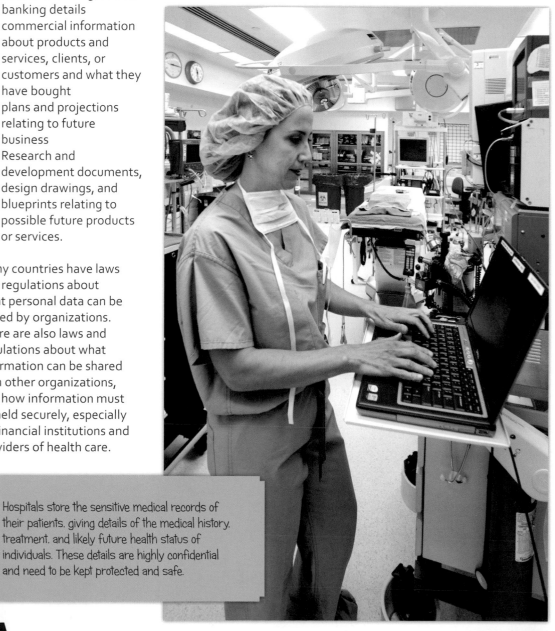

Hospitals store the sensitive medical records of their patients, giving details of the medical history, treatment, and likely future health status of individuals. These details are highly confidential and need to be kept protected and safe.

Protecting data

Organizations must protect their own commercial and financial data, so that competitors do not gain advantages over them, perhaps stealing product ideas or luring away customers. They also have a legal duty to protect the personal and financial details of employees and customers.

Lena finds that Ben's account has been used to change the organization's web site and to clear a lot of outstanding customer debts. She has to ask the accounts department to check the debt clearance, since data protection legislation does not allow her to look at the personal financial accounts of customers. She is very worried that customers' financial details have been compromised. This is a serious security breach and could lead to legal problems.

Financial details must be kept secure to prevent fraud or theft. Individuals have a responsibility to keep their own details safe. but organizations that store financial records have to safeguard them. too.

Data protection laws

Many countries have laws requiring organizations that store personal details to register with a special body and carefully protect the data. In the United States, there is a collection of federal and state laws and self-regulation measures.

There are also restrictions on what organizations can do with personal data. They have to tell you what they will do with the information, and then they must not use it for other purposes. They are not allowed to share or sell it without your permission, and they must keep it secure.

If you register with a band's web site to get updates about its tour dates, the web site should not use your details for anything else. Carefully read the text beside all the checkboxes— some web sites use confusing wording to get you to agree to share or sell your details.

YOU'RE THE INVESTIGATOR!: THE ANSWER

The following lines are suspicious:

H:\root\user\web\pages\offers\june.html	03:01:04	delete
H:\root\user\web\pages\offers\top.html	03:01:05	delete
H:\root\user\web\pages\offers\today.html	03:01:06	delete
H:\root\user\web\pages\contact\mailto.html	03:01:08	update
H:\root\user\web\pages\offers\june.html	03:01:11	upload
H:\ProgramData\Sage\Accounts\2014	05:38:26	update

Ben's responsibilities do not include changing the web site, or the web pages. He does not normally work at three o'clock in the morning. This is not Ben's normal activity, and when asked about it, he says he did not change these files.

Forensic Computing

Once it is obvious that the cyber attack is serious enough to be treated as a criminal offense, the organization Ben works for involves the police. The police want to solve the crime and also stop any further damage. They work quickly to protect the organization from additional risk as they investigate.

Who did it?

It can be very difficult to figure out who is responsible for a cyber attack. The attacker could be anywhere in the world, and the only evidence is a trail of changed data. The police experts use deductive skills, software tools, and advanced knowledge of computers to figure out where the attack came from and what exactly has happened.

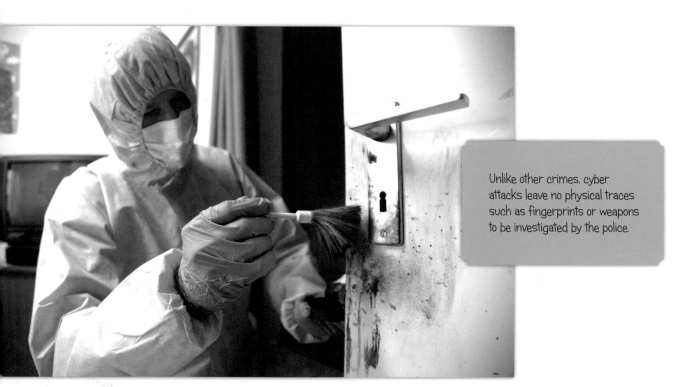

Unlike other crimes, cyber attacks leave no physical traces such as fingerprints or weapons to be investigated by the police.

Collecting evidence

A police investigator, Stephanie, visits and copies all the files and logs that might be useful for the investigation. She explains to Greg that the entries in the log files show the attacker is not an expert—a very good hacker would have deleted entries from the log files afterward. She also takes Ben's laptop away for **forensics** experts (see the box on page 37) to examine.

COMPUTER FORENSICS EXPERT

Computer forensics experts can work for the police or a private company. They must follow rigorous procedures and document every step of the investigation carefully, because their work might be needed as evidence in a court case.

The expert first secures the system and disconnects it from the Internet, preventing any further changes to files. Even opening a file can change it, so the forensics expert must work only on copies. The expert retrieves deleted and hidden files, decodes encrypted files (files that have been converted into special code), and opens files protected by passwords. All are copied.

Forensics experts need an excellent knowledge of how computer systems and malware work. They must also know how to use special software tools to recover and examine files.

Police forensics workers take away all the evidence. bagging and cataloging physical evidence.

Computers on the Internet

When a computer connects to the Internet, it identifies itself by giving its **IP address**, short for "Internet protocol" address (see page 38). If it did not do this, it could not receive any information—just as you cannot receive any letters if you do not tell anyone your postal address. There is a record of communications between IP addresses that forensics experts can use to help track down cyber criminals. It is like a burglar leaving a card with his address on it in a house he robbed!

IP addresses

An IP address is a string of numbers that identifies the computer: four sets of numbers 0–255, separated by dots, such as 173.17.254.0. This format can provide 4,294,967,296 numbers, but that is no longer enough. A new form of IP address has been introduced that allows for far more numbers—2^{128}, or around 3 followed by 38 zeroes!

With the right equipment or browser settings, it is possible to see the IP address of a computer that is connected online, wherever it is. If a person uses a computer in an Internet café, they can be traced because the café will have logged who used the computer.

The police investigators can see—from the log file—the IP address of the person who changed the files. Although the hacker used Ben's login details, this person used his or her own computer, and so that IP address has been recorded.

Tracking an IP address

Internet service providers (ISPs) distribute IP addresses. The police can find out from the ISP who had the particular IP address used for the attack and then track the hacker. But Stephanie knows she has to act quickly, because IP addresses change, and the ISP might not keep its records of old IP addresses for long. Luckily, the ISP gives her the customer's street address.

Identifying the computer does not show who used it for the attack, though. In addition, a skilled hacker can route communications through a series of other computers, all with different IP addresses. There is not always a log of these communications.

Every item that accesses the Internet has its own IP address, including every tablet, smartphone, and laptop.

The IP address is only ever likely to be secondary evidence—the police will need something else to prove that an individual carried out the crime. They will need to use conventional police techniques, such as questioning and looking for fingerprints and telltale files on the computer used for the attack.

Hacking and the law

Hacking is illegal in many countries. In the United States, it is covered by the Computer Fraud and Abuse Act (1986), which regulates against:
- accessing computers without authorization
- distributing malware
- trafficking in passwords or other means of accessing computers without authorization.

Worldwide web of crime

The Internet is a global network—a hacker can work in one country to attack computers in another. Police forces in different countries often have to work together to solve cyber crimes. In the United States, the Federal Bureau of Investigation (FBI) has Cyber Action Teams (CATs). These are highly trained teams of FBI agents, analysts, and experts in computer forensics and malware. They travel around the world to respond to suspected cyber crime attacks, taking enough hardware, software, and forensics equipment to be self-supporting. **Extradition** treaties between some countries mean that hackers can be sent to the country in which the law was broken to be tried and punished.

Gary McKinnon

In 2001-2002, Scottish system administrator Gary McKinnon hacked into 97 U.S. military and NASA computers. McKinnon said he was looking for evidence of UFOs covered up by the U.S. authorities. In 2005, the United States began extradition proceedings. The case has caused international discussion. McKinnon, who is **autistic**, could have been jailed for up to 70 years in the United States. Finally, in 2012, the British government blocked his extradition because of serious concerns about his health.

Finding the malware

Forensic experts look at Ben's computer to find the malware. They use special software to scan the computer for keylogging software, and they examine the registry to find entries that show there is extra software installed that is not part of the operating system or any of the applications Ben has installed. These checks show several bits of malware, including a keylogger and the original Trojan. If the Trojan were a new, unknown one, an expert computer programmer could be employed to reverse engineer it, figuring out from the computer code what the malware is doing.

THE WORLDWIDE FIGHT AGAINST A SCAM

"Scareware" is characterized by pop-up messages saying the computer has a virus or other problem that can be fixed by buying a piece of advertised software. People who fall victim to the scam pay to download malware and might have their credit card details stolen. The threat mentioned in the message does not exist, and the download is of no value or use.

In 2011, the FBI traced a scareware scam to the Ukraine. The Security Service of Ukraine used over 100 officers and worked with the German BKA, Latvian State Police, and Cyprus National Police to track the criminals, who were based in Kyiv, Ukraine. In all, law enforcement agencies of 12 countries were involved in cracking the crime ring, seizing servers, and arresting the criminals.

One of the scams involved tricking computer users into downloading a piece of software which claimed it would scan their computers for viruses, but in fact installed malware. In fact, there was nothing wrong with the computer until the user downloaded the fake security software. The FBI believes as many as 960,000 people fell victim to the scam and lost a total of $72 million.

Anti-forensics tricks

Accomplished hackers can make the work of investigators very difficult. They can use software tools to break up a file or to program and hide parts inside several other files. They can also change the header data (the data at the start of the file that tells the computer what to expect), making one type of file look like another. They can change the date the file was created or accessed. For instance, a file with a fake creation date, set in the future, is hard to find, because the computer does not list it among current files. Forensics experts have to be aware of these kinds of tactics and make sure they do not damage or miss any evidence.

These are some of the computers and equipment used in a New York City cyber crime lab.

Motive and method

In the case of Ben's computer, the police visit the address they have been given by the ISP and seize a laptop. Its owner is a previous employee of the organization who had lost his job. Forensics investigators examine the laptop and find the code for a Trojan that matches the one on Ben's laptop. The man had e-mailed Ben a small game, which Ben had opened and run because he knew and trusted the man. This had installed the Trojan, along with a keylogger, which sent everything Ben typed to the hacker—including the login details for the organization's network.

Flyby attack

The changes to Ben's social network and e-mail accounts were made from a different IP address, though. The police decide these changes were a separate, opportunistic attack.

A **port** is a software connection on a computer for sending or receiving information. Much like the different channels on a TV, the computer uses different ports for different communications. A Trojan leaves a port open on a computer. This means that traffic can go between the computer and Internet, bypassing the firewall. Casual hackers often use special software to scan the Internet for computers with open ports and then steal information, launch attacks, install malware, or take over computers as zombies. The police believe an opportunistic hacker noticed the open port on Ben's laptop, sent e-mail from his account, and changed his social network status and passwords.

How computer programs work

A computer program is a set of instructions written in a special "language," or code, such as C++ or VB.NET. When a programmer has finished writing the instructions, the program is compiled, meaning it is processed to become the number-based code that computers can understand.

A fragment of computer code looks meaningless to anyone who cannot understand that particular computer language, but to experienced programmers it is a series of instructions.

A Secure Future

After the police have finished their work, Ben's organization can restore its system and make it secure for the future. This time, they have been lucky—no serious harm has been done. But they are eager to protect their systems from more damaging attacks in the future.

Restoring the system

The files that have been changed must be restored to their correct state. Lena, the network manager, restores the last good versions of the files from backup copies. A backup is an extra copy of a file kept in case something goes wrong with the working copy. It is needed if a file is accidentally or deliberately deleted or ruined, or if the computer stops working.

DATA RECOVERY EXPERT

If important files are overwritten or deleted, or disks are damaged, data recovery experts can often restore the lost information.

Data recovery experts, also called recovery engineers, work with hardware or software failures. They need engineering and computing skills, a good knowledge of computer systems and programming, and the ability to work under pressure. They work to retrieve data from computers damaged by fire or flood or even those that have been crushed or vandalized. They also work with computers that have simply stopped working. These services are very expensive and are used mostly by businesses.

Keeping backups

Most organizations use two types of backup. A disaster recovery backup is a copy of the entire system, and it is used if the whole computer system is destroyed. Making this type of backup is expensive and time-consuming—you could not do it every day! It is kept in a different physical location so that it is not destroyed in the same disaster that destroys the main system.

Smaller backups are made more frequently, often every day. These rolling backups are extra copies of files that change between the major backups.

KEEP YOUR DATA SAFE

You should back up your own work on your school or home computer. You can store your information on a memory stick, another disk drive on the network, or an online cloud computing backup service, which uses remote servers hosted on the Internet. Make a full backup of your system, and then make backups of your important files when you change them. Once you have set a backup location, many computers let you use a setting to make backups automatically.

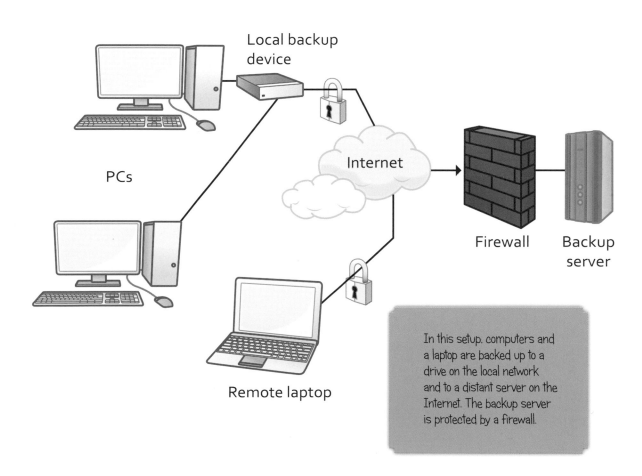

Local backup device

PCs

Internet

Firewall

Backup server

Remote laptop

In this setup, computers and a laptop are backed up to a drive on the local network and to a distant server on the Internet. The backup server is protected by a firewall.

Identifying weak points

Greg calls in computer security experts to look carefully at the system and identify weak points and then suggest ways of increasing security. Computer security is a special area of expertise. He calls on a penetration tester—also known as a legal hacker, or a "white hat" hacker.

Making the system secure

Security experts suggest how Ben's organization can protect the computer system in the future. All laptops that are used to access the organization's network must have anti-malware software that is automatically updated and also have a robust firewall in place for all Internet access. The organization's computers all have antivirus software, and the firewall is strengthened. Employees are trained in safe computer use. This is an important measure, as human carelessness can make even the best-designed system vulnerable.

Education is an important part of computer security. Hackers often depend on the ignorance or carelessness of users.

PENETRATION TESTER

Penetration testers try to attack the system as a hacker would, looking for weak points that give entry to the network. They report to the organization employing them on the security loopholes they find, and they help the organization to block off those routes, making the system secure against genuine attacks.

Most penetration testers are expert computer programmers with an interest in security. Some have previously been recreational or criminal hackers, but they have decided to put their skills to good, legal use. They use the tools and expertise available to hackers and try attacks that could be malicious, or that might result from curiosity or a sense of challenge.

To prevent interfering with a working system, penetration testers sometimes work on a cloned system—an exact copy of the computer system—or at night and on weekends, when the computers are not used much.

Facing the future

In this case, the organization has learned a lot from the cyber attack and has not suffered greatly. It has been lucky—the consequences could have been a lot more serious. Instead, the IT department has been given the chance to review and strengthen its security measures, making it a much more difficult target for any future hackers.

The organization decides to keep better control of laptops and other mobile devices connecting to the internal network. All laptops and tablets will have up-to-date security software installed by the IT department. Each device that is to be used to connect to the network must be registered with the IT department and checked for malware before being used the first time, and at regular intervals thereafter. When anyone leaves, the IT department will change any passwords they once knew.

Investigation: How to Be Anonymous

Computer systems often deal with anonymized data, which is information stored in a way that does not link it to people. For example, people often respond to a survey or allow their data to be used as long as it cannot be traced back to them. In some countries where Internet use is restricted, people use anonymizing systems to hide their use of banned political or religious web sites.

Many web sites collect information about the people who use the site. This helps companies to target their content or products to their audience. But people are rightly wary about giving away too much information about themselves.

This investigation shows how it is possible to come up with ways to keep data anonymous.

The challenge

Imagine that a music web site called MonsterMusic wants to sell music downloads to 13-year-olds, so it wants to know how much (if anything) 13-year-olds receive as an allowance. Carol from MonsterMusic goes to a school to meet 100 students who are the right age. But the students will not tell her how much they receive for their allowances. Carol needs a way to let people keep their personal information secret.

WHAT TO DO

Try this with your classmates to see how you can solve Carol's problem.

Give each person a blank piece of paper. Tell the first person to think of a sum of money between $5 and $15 and add his or her allowance to it, then write the total on the paper and pass it to the next person. That person adds his or her allowance to the total, writes it on his or her own piece of paper, and passes it on.

Suppose when the last person gives you the piece of paper, the figure on it is $1,060.42. Now ask yourself the following questions:

Question 1: What information do you need to know in order to figure out the average allowance for this group of people?

Question 2: If you were told the missing piece of information is $7.30, how would you figure out the average? What is the average?

Question 3: If any of the students compared their pieces of paper, without knowing the order in which they were written, would they be able to figure out how much someone else received as an allowance, assuming no one is prepared to reveal his or her own allowance?

A sum of money between $5 and $15

$7.30 + $11 = $18.30

The first person's allowance

$18.30 + $8.50 = $26.80

$26.80 + $11 = $37.80

$37.80 + $9.20 = $47.00

$18.30

$26.80

$37.80

$47.00

This diagram shows how each person adds their allowance to the number they are given. and then passes the new number to the next person.

Answers

Answer 1: You would need to know how much the first person added to his or her allowance.

Answer 2: If the amount added by the first person is $7.30, and the amount on the last piece of paper is $1,060.42, this is the way to find the average:
$1,060.42 − $7.30 = $1,053.12 (total allowance for the whole group)
$1,053.12 ÷ 100 students = $10.53 per student (the average)

Answer 3: Without knowing the order the numbers were written in, no student could figure out any other's allowance and be sure of the answer.
Imagine the amount on Abigail's paper is $234.00. Mustafa tells her his amount is $285.00. Abigail can figure out that $285 − $234 = $51. This tells her that Mustafa's allowance cannot be more than $51, because that is how much has been added between her writing on her paper and Mustafa writing on his—although there could have been several people between them.

But if the amount Mustafa wrote down was $240.00, the difference would be only $6, and Abigail might guess that Mustafa gets $6 for his allowance.

Timeline

A cyber attack is not always discovered as soon as it happens. If the hacker wants the assault to stay hidden—perhaps while he or she continues to drain information from the system or hijack it—the attack may go unnoticed for weeks, months, or even years. The investigation only begins when someone notices that something is wrong...

Hour 0

Ben notices something suspicious in the way his computer is behaving and in some files that have been changed.

Hour 1

If an attack is suspected, the system is secured—if possible. This might involve changing passwords, logging out of systems, and disconnecting from the Internet. This is to prevent further access and possible damage.

Days 1–2

As soon as possible, an IT expert such as a system administrator looks at the system to confirm the attack. Over the next few hours, the expert tries to figure out which parts of the system have been damaged or accessed.

Days 3+

If an attack is serious, the system administrator might call in the police.

Police investigators will take away laptops and removable drives that have been affected and will take copies of all the files on the affected system. This can take a long time, as some systems are very large. The police have a lot of crimes to deal with. More serious crimes will be treated as urgent, and lesser crimes might be dealt with more slowly if resources are limited.

Days 3+

Forensics experts use their knowledge and software tools to examine disk drives and files for clues. They look at log files to see when files have been accessed and who has accessed them. They investigate disks, looking for hidden, disguised, or deleted files that might be malware or might give a clue to illegal activity. This part of the investigation can take days, weeks, or even months.

If the police can use IP addresses or other clues to lead them to particular computers used in an attack, they will visit the physical address with a search warrant that enables them to seize or search the computer equipment they believe was used in the attack. They then examine the seized computers, looking for files and other traces that link it with the attack. If they find matching data or files, they can pass the case to prosecutors, and then the suspect will be arrested.

The future of cyber crime

For a long time, most malware targeted PCs running Windows and often the browser Internet Explorer. Since around 2010, the scope of malware has increased, attacking other browsers on PCs and also Apple computers running MacOS and browsers including Firefox, Opera, and Safari. As people use a wider variety of devices to connect to the Internet and to store and move data, malware for these is appearing.

Glossary

activist someone who takes drastic or direct action to bring attention to a cause they believe in

application software used to carry out a particular task, such as create documents or work with photos

autistic having a mind differently organized from many people, which can lead to good skills in ordering and logic, but difficulties with communication and relating to other people

botnet network of computers that have been taken over, usually without their owners' knowledge or permission, and used for cyber attacks

compromised made vulnerable

data details or information, such as text, numbers, and pictures

distributed denial-of-service (DDoS) attack on a computer system carried out by getting lots of computers to try to access the same server or web site at the same time

download (used as both noun and verb) file copied from the Internet onto a local computer; the act of copying a file from the Internet onto a computer

extradition sending someone out of a country to face trial for a crime in another country

firewall software or hardware that screens data going between a computer system or network and the Internet, intended to keep the local computer or network safe

forensic relating to the investigation of crimes

hack (used as both noun and verb) attack on a computer system; to carry out an attack on a computer system by breaking into it remotely over the Internet

hacker a person who illegally breaks into computer systems over the Internet

hardware the physical components of a computer system

identity theft use of someone's personal details without their permission, usually in order to carry out crimes

infect compromise a computer system by installing malware

Internet service provider (ISP) organization that provides a link to the Internet for home or business computer users

IP address series of numbers that identifies a computer connected to the Internet

keylogger a piece of software which records every key press of a computer keyboard

log file file that lists activity on a computer

malware software created to cause harm, such as viruses and worms

modem device for connecting a computer to the Internet

network system of computers joined together in order to share resources and files

operating system software that controls how a computer operates

port connector

process activity running on a computer

registry part of the Windows operating system that stores information about and for programs installed on the computer

router hardware to control data moving between computers on a network or between computers and the Internet

server computer that delivers files or services to other computers on a network

software computer programs

spam unwanted email sent out as a bulk mailing

spyware software that spies on computer activity and sends reports of it to a distant computer over the Internet

Trojan malware that has been smuggled onto a computer with other software

virus disruptive or destructive software that spreads between computers in shared files and disks

worm disruptive or destructive software that spreads between networked computers

zombie a computer that has been taken over and controlled remotely as part of a botnet

Find Out More

Books

Goldsmith, Mike, and Tom Jackson. *Computer* (Eyewitness). New York: Dorling Kindersley, 2011.

Hynson, Colin. *Cyber Crime* (Inside Crime). Mankato, Minn.: Smart Apple Media, 2012.

Townsend, John. *Cyber Crime Secrets* (Amazing Crime Scene Science). Mankato, Minn.: Amicus, 2012.

Anderson, M.T. *Feed*. London: Walker Books, 2003.

Set in the future when most people have an implant that connects them permanently to the Internet, two teens meet and start a relationship when their Feeds are hacked.

Doctorow, Cory. *Little Brother*. New York: Harper Voyager, 2008.

A teen hacker is arrested after a terrorist attack on San Francisco. After his release, he decides to bring down the surveillance state. Free download from Cory Doctorow's website: http://craphound.com/littlebrother/download/.

Rose, Malcolm. *Jordan Stryker: Cyber Terror*. London: Usborne, 2011.

Unit Red agent Jordan Stryker battles against a cyber terrorist assault that could destroy the world.

Wasserman, Robin. *Hacking Harvard*. New York: Simon Pulse, 2007.

Eric, Max, and Schwarz are teen hackers who set out to get a third-rate student into Harvard by hacking into the admissions computer system.

Web sites

www.cybercitizenship.org
The Cybercitizen Awareness Program works to educate young people about the dangers of cyber crime, while also teaching young people how to protect themselves from these kinds of attacks.

www.fbi.gov/about-us/investigate/cyber/cyber
This FBI web site is full of up-to-the-minute information about cyber crime and how the FBI aggressively pursues these crimes. It includes a list of threats and scams to look out for as well as ways to protect yourself.

www.youtube.com/watch?v=tfv5JASJxbA
This is a CNN simulation of how a massive cyber attack might have an impact on the United States. (This is the first of nine short parts.)

Movies

War Games (United Artists, 1983)
In this movie, a teenage boy finds a "backdoor" into a U.S. military computer system and begins a dangerous game that could start World War III.

Hackers, 1995

A boy is banned from using the Internet until he is 18 after writing a computer virus. He and his friends discover a plot to release a dangerous computer virus, and race to find evidence of it before either the Secret Service or the evil virus-writer stop them.

Other topics to research

If you enjoyed this book, you might like to research these other topics:

- Cyber terrorism: A sophisticated cyber attack could damage a large business organization or even compromise a country or its national security. Find out what can be done to guard against this, and what a serious attack might be able to achieve.

- One step ahead: People who work on computer security try to stay one step ahead of criminals by figuring out what they might do and preventing it. Research the work of computer security experts.

- "Black hat" to "white hat": Find out about how "white hat" hackers work using "black hat" techniques, and learn about the value of their work.

Index